Real Estate Investing

50 Tips To Get You Started In Successful Real Estate Investing

By Ezra Carter

Copyright @2017

All rights reserved. No part of this book may be reproduced in any form or by any means without permission in writing from the publisher.

This book is produced with the goal of providing information that is as accurate and reliable as possible. Regardless, purchasing this book can be seen as consent to the fact that both the publisher and the author of this book are in no way experts on the topics discussed within and that any recommendations or suggestions that are made herein are for entertainment purposes only. Professionals should be consulted as needed prior to undertaking any of the action endorsed herein.

This declaration is deemed fair and valid by both the American Bar Association and the Committee of Publishers Association and is legally binding throughout the United States.

Furthermore, the transmission, duplication or reproduction of any of the following work including specific information will be considered an illegal act irrespective of if it is done electronically or in print. This extends to creating a secondary or tertiary copy of the work or a recorded copy and is only allowed with express written consent from the Publisher. All additional right reserved.

The information in the following pages is broadly considered to be a truthful and accurate account of facts and as such any inattention, use or misuse of the information in question by the reader will render any resulting actions solely under their purview. There are no scenarios in which the publisher or the original author of this work can be in any fashion deemed liable for any hardship or damages that may befall them after undertaking information described herein.

Additionally, the information in the following pages is intended only for informational purposes and should thus be thought of as universal. As befitting its nature, it is presented without assurance regarding its prolonged validity or interim quality. Trademarks that are mentioned are done without written consent and can in no way be considered an endorsement from the trademark holder.

If you like my book, please leave a positive review on Amazon. I would appreciate it a lot. Thanks!

Contents:

Introduction

Chapter 1: The Basics of Real Estate Investing

Chapter 2: Beginning Your Journey in Real Estate Investing

Chapter 3: 9 Tips to Get You Started in Real Estate Investing

Chapter 4: How to Choose Your Niche in Real Estate Investing

Chapter 5: Choose Your Real Estate Investing Strategies

Chapter 6: Resources & Tools for the Newbie Investor

Chapter 7: How to Avoid Common Mistakes Newbie Investors Make

Chapter 8: The Correct Way to Value and Analyze Investment Property

Conclusion

Introduction

You have most likely heard about real estate on and off. By acquiring this book, you are probably thinking of investing in real estate for the first time, or you have the means to invest and would like some necessary information before you begin somewhere.

Firstly, real estate means property which can be in the form of land or a building, and everything else within that said land or building. Real estate investing is the activity centered on making profits from a tangible piece of real estate.

Real estate investing is one of the earliest methods of investments. It has been around since the beginning of human civilization, and back in the days, real estate investing by emperors and monarchies came in the form of conquering lands and colonizing them.

Back to modern times, real estate investing is among the five basic asset classes- shares, bonds, property, commodities and cash and it is a form of investing that is among the most attractive in an investor's portfolio because of its profitability, unique cash flow, and liquidity as well as diversification benefits.

This book will cover everything about guiding new investors in the art of real estate investing. We will be walking over the basics and giving you some in-depth content to the various useful concepts in real estate and also tips and ideas on how to invest in the right property, mistakes to avoid, tax advantages and so on.

But first, the basics.

Chapter 1: The Basics of Real Estate Investing

What is Real Estate Investing?

As mentioned earlier on, real estate investing is the financial activity of operating and investing from a material property, and there are plenty of ways that a person can procure cash flow other than just buying a property and renting it.

The most fundamental form of real estate investing is the investor, otherwise known as the landlord. The landlord purchases a piece of tangible assets, and this can be any property whether a land with a house on it, or just a land, a raw farmland, a land with a building on it or a warehouse on it- it doesn't matter what the type is. Once the landlord acquires said piece of land, she then finds ways of utilizing the property and usually, it is finding someone who may want to use this property. This someone is known as the tenant.

If both parties agree on renting, leasing or using the property in a certain way, they enter into an agreement. This agreement is called a lease contract or rental agreement. The tenant is then given access to the property or land, and he can use it according to the agreed terms, and according to the agreed length of time. The tenant, in exchange for using your property, pays for the use and this is usually called the rent. Okay- that's the basic, purely fundamental activity of real estate investing. You buy a property and lease or rent it out. You are paid in rental money by the tenant.

For many property owners and investors, real estate investing has a huge psychological advantage compared to investing in bonds and stocks. Real estate investing is a hugely popular form for many investors because investors can drive by their property, touch it, see it, walk inside it, and take pictures of it-- the whole nine yards. The thing is, sometimes real estate investors can become misguided just like stock investors, especially when the stock market bubbles and when this happens, the investor can insist that capitalization rates don't matter.

In a manner of speaking, when an investor can set a price for rental appropriately, then he would be able to enjoy a satisfactory ROI (Return On Investment) on his capital after subtracting the cost of the property, income and property taxes, insurance, maintenance costs and other expenditures. Additionally, always remember that time is your most valuable asset. Calculate the amount of time you need to deal with your investment- this is the reason why passive income is ever so relevant to investors.

Types of Real Estate Investments

One of the key things to do when you start out in real estate is to find your niche. Your niche should be something that you are familiar with. If you are familiar with townhouses, then start there. If you are comfortable with warehouses- begin there. Whatever you do, there are plenty of options in property investments that you can look at that are above and beyond what you are comfortable and familiar with so it could be something to look into once you get the hang of investing.

The major categories of real estate properties are organized according to its unique advantages and disadvantages, its economic distinctiveness and rental sequence, brokerage practices as well as common lease terms. Here are some of the common categories of real estate that you will find in almost any country:

- Residential real estate
- Commercial real estate
- Industrial real estate
- Retail real estate
- Mixed-use real estate

Another way you can get involved in real estate investing is by way of lending:

- You can own a bank that does underwriting of mortgages and commercial real estate loans
- You can provide underwriting private mortgages for individuals, which usually comes at high-interest rates to compensate for the additional risk
- You can also invest in something called mezzanine securities, which allows you to loan money to a real estate development which you can then exchange into equity possession

Apart from the above, you can also do an extension of real estate investing which is:

- Letting a space so that you have minimum capital tied up in it, enhancing it and then sub-leasing that same exact space to other people for a higher rental rate. This creates incredible returns on capital. An example of space could be a flexible office business venue that allows mobile workers to buy or rent office time

- Obtaining tax-lien certificates. These are a hidden part of real estate investing and not recommended for hands-off or untrained investors. However, with the right conditions and acting at the precise time, with the right sort of person, it will produce high returns

But above all, the most common real estate investment mostly done by a lot of individuals with significant income would be to own a house and then rent it out.

Chapter 2: Beginning Your Journey in Real Estate Investing

Opportunity is out there- it's how you look at these prospects. Some people look at the glass half full, and some look at it as a glass half empty, others ask where the faucet is. For example, a long and harsh winter spells doom for some, but for those looking to make profitable investments can spell low-interest rates and a high demand for rentals. In other words, it smells like opportunity.

Real estate investing is sort of like going to war. You need luck, you also need a strategy, you need good mentors, and you also need to wait for the right opportunity to strike. Buying and selling real estate requires some sense of fundamentals as well as basic approaches and strategies. You can use a combination of strategies, and you can also just stick with one.

The experienced investor knows that different properties require different strategies.

When it comes to real estate investing, there are two basic approaches that you can use to steer yourself.

i. **Buying shares in a real estate investment trust (REIT)**

By investing in a REIT, that would also mean you are required to buy shares of a range of properties. Investing in REIT is like buying stocks or buying funds. It is a completely different scenario compared to buying the hard cold real estate. Gary Gastineau, the founder of ETF Consultants, says that when it comes to real estate, there are essentially three layers of value- the real estate itself, the cash flow and the management that supports the trust and finally, the funds based on the trust.

A portfolio with REIT added to it can complement bond funds and stocks, but an investor must understand how real estate funds are designed how their manager will extract value from its holdings. You can purchase shares of REITs and real estate based funds, but the performance of these funds is largely based on a combination of cash flow and gains from the occasional buying and selling of properties. This is an entirely different scenario from the common climate that drives stock and bond funds.

ii. Direct Ownership of Real Estate

Direct ownership is anything but a passive investment. Plenty of people think that direct ownership of property means easy money and there's not plenty of work involved and that their tenants will pay on time or that the roof doesn't crack and the pipes don't leak.

Many people enter real estate investing by starting small, buying a little apartment building or a small flat. However, a wise advice from Gary Gastineau is to do some research to find an excellent deal on a building that will provide some positive cash flow, and hopefully one that has no hidden defects that will eat into this cash flow and result in expensive repairs. Buying a small flat or apartment building will not do much for your investment portfolio if it's a dormant piece of investment with no foreseeable cash flow. There has to be a tenant, or a guarantee of one. HOA's (home owner associations) will also eat into your monthly cash flow and those should be avoided when possible.

Gary also warns not to take investment advice from a real estate agent. To real estate agents, everything is a good investment because they get commissions when you buy. Also, just because you have experience as a homeowner, doesn't make you an expert on a larger scale. Home-owning rentals are so different compared to large scale building rentals.

There are different regulations concerning homes or business units. There are various insurance-related matters, building codes and yes, safety guidelines. Managing a bigger scale property takes away your time and money.

Thinking of managing a large property? Well, perhaps you can start with buying a duplex or a tiny low-density apartment building, with the aim of living in one unit and renting the rest, then see how your tolerance level is by managing maintenance, upkeep, security, and safety as well as the good old rent.

While this is a good idea, you may set yourself up with a high learning curve and play dual roles- that of a first-time owner and a first-time landlord. Up for it? Before you say yes, some fundamental idea of what real estate investing entails, the rental rates, market prices and so on is beneficial.

Most importantly, you need to understand that today's rising rental rates will not necessarily lift future cash flow. The rental market of today will gradually alleviate when projects that were under construction open up for purchase which means that rents will level off. In this scenario, it is best to work your cash flow and return numbers using conservative projections.

Cash flow key factors involve not only predictable costs but also variables that can ultimately affect the appeal of your property units to potential renters. Say for an instant, you think adding heating and water, and some furniture will attract tenants. However, if your tenants use more water and heat, this ultimately means less money for you to keep.

There are new tools that can help a new landlord with guidance, resources and some fantastic data that can be used to calculate costs and returns of buying properties for investment purposes.

The TLCEngine is an excellent tool to estimate the 'true lifestyle cost' when you own property. When you do a spreadsheet of home ownership, you look into values such as principal and interest. The TLCEngine looks at other factors as well such as utilities, commuting costs and the distance of common services such as schools and hospitals that will affect the cost of living in your property. These factors can help you figure out how much you will be required to spend a month if you live in your purchased property. This data will ultimately help you market your property to potential renters, and help you make better, informed decisions.

Founder and CEO of TLCEngine, Krishna Malyala realized this invention when he and his wife were struggling to figure out how much it would cost them to purchase properties that they were considering. Malyala, a financial data analyst before becoming CEO, created a spreadsheet that enables him to calculate the relative costs of owning a piece of property and when he did this, he realized that other potential property owners would be interested in it as well.

Currently, this tool specifically caters to agents and multiple listing agents, but he's working on a consumer-friendly version as well.

Another tool that can help potential landlords is called Down Payment Resource. With this tool, buyers can find programs that can help them with a down payment. Buyers and lenders can use this service to find applicable and appropriate programs with the down payment. Rob Crane, founder of Down Payment Resource, stresses that plenty of programs include owner-occupied properties for up to four units which give way for first-time buyers to build on their equity and capture income as well.

Chapter 3: 9 Tips to Get You Started in Real Estate Investing

Some of these tips are pretty common sense but then again, it's always good to remind yourself why you are getting yourself into real-estate investing, even if you are a pro at it.

1- Understand that your investments are a business, so plan for it

Getting into real estate is going to be a business, whether you like it to be or not. Even if you only buy one property- it is a business of managing it since it takes up part of your life. So before buying, take your investment seriously and plan for your future.

2- Find someone who knows more than you do

Find someone with experience in real estate investing to understand the inner workings of real estate and make them your mentor. Attend seminars and workshops if you have to because you need to know everything important from new construction to tear downs, renovation rates, and fires. Acquire as much knowledge and understanding of the business you are getting into, through the eyes and ears and experiences of people who have been there, done that. When you do run into problems- call your mentor to get some advice. You do not have to know everything yourself.

3- Invest for the purpose of cash flow

Before anything else- make sure your numbers on the spreadsheet workout. You must buy property for cash flow and just not speculate that the assets 'will appreciate in the next five years.' Nope. Don't do that. Instead, use the tools mentioned above to calculate the various factors that will appreciate your property and to what rate. A lot of internet sites and even real estate agents will tell you that properties, no matter where will appreciate. But what they don't tell you is how fast. But at the end of the day, it is pretty common sense to understand which areas of your city or region appreciate fast and which do not.

Your cash flow needs to work because even if the market tanked, you would still be able to stay afloat and over the long term period, you would see the appreciation. Buy where the numbers work.

4- Invest in your knowledge

Take your time to gather industry knowledge before and while you invest. You are bound to learn new things on the way. Learn from your mistakes and build on experience. Apart from learning things from books, read articles online, speak to real-estate gurus and take some classes in accountancy and finance- just to help you along the way. Read real-estate books from Kiyosaki and Trump- just keep learning.

5- Get yourself started

No amount of research and reading will make you completely ready and full-proof unless you put your knowledge to good use. You will never be able to use the knowledge that you have unless you take the plunge and seriously start investing. Sure- start small. That is where all of us started anyway.

6- Explore your niche

Finding your focus is key, especially when you are starting out. There is no point in trying to be all kinds of things. Focus on areas that you are familiar with that would give you a better of the properties in this field, the distances of the schools, hospitals and transportation hubs, upcoming commercial projects that will provide value to that area and access to shopping malls or even local attractions. This will give you some foresight of whether the properties would appreciate.

You can also focus on properties to a select target age such as millennial tenants or students looking to rent or older senior citizens looking to purchase a retirement home. You can also look at either high-end rentals or affordable housing rentals. The key here is to start a focus before you diversify your interests.

7- Anticipate problems

The path to glory is paved with broken glasses. Nobody said that it would be easy. If you are not facing any problems, you are probably not doing it right or not making a significant move. In any business, you are bound to be facing problems, and it is a process of solving one problem after the next. How you address these problems will teach you to be a better real estate investor when the opportunity comes for you purchase even more important properties.

8- Do not think you are going to get rich quick

The faster you acquire money, the faster you will lose it. If you are starting out in real estate (or virtually anything in particular), do not expect to be a know-it-all and do not expect to be rich so fast. Real estate investing is not a 'get rich overnight' scheme, rather it's a gradual and satisfactory process towards getting rich. It takes hard work, it takes know-how, it takes time and patience, and it also takes instinct.

9- Stay focused

This may sound cheesy but you need to keep your eye on the prize. This will help you design your own destiny and create your own niche. By working hard and hanging on even, when times are rough, eventually you will get to afford the lifestyle that you want. Focusing on a set of properties with good cash flow, keeping to your niche when you start will help you expand your network and connections and eventually help you branch out to other interesting prospects in the real estate market.

Chapter 4: How to Choose Your Niche in Real Estate Investing

There are plenty of ways to make money in real estate, and ultimately, it all begins with figuring out what niche works best for you and what doesn't. Finding your niche makes your investment journey unique but also a lot easier. But how do you find your niche?

You may like or feel comfortable working on certain niches and strategies, and there are some that you avoid at all costs. As an investor, you get to access the variety of choices available to you, before you settle on a particular niche that you enjoy dealing and managing with.

It's best not to work in all niches. Instead, learning how to invest in real estate successfully is all about choosing a niche and becoming the master of it. In this chapter, we will discuss how to choose your niche.

Choosing your niche helps your narrow your focus point and become an expert. It will also enable you to grow your network with the people within that niche, and you can start building your wealth by making a plan, taking action and executing your plan.

Picking Your Real Estate Investment Niche

Here we have listed some of the most common property types that most investors deal with and it will most likely be something that you, a newbie investor can try your hands at doing. Each of these listings has its own extensions, but you don't need to know them all. This list is primarily to help you get your bearings and see the different options available.

- **Raw Land**

Raw land refers to a piece of land without a building, plantation or any other human-made element on it. With this land, you can improve it to attach value, or it can be loan or rented out to make cash flow. Raw land can also be separated and sold. Investors decide to purchase raw land with the aspiration and plan to trade it in for something more valuable such as for development or construction for a freeway.

- **Single-Family Homes**

This is by far the most common forms of real estate investment that most first time investors go for. Single family homes are a favorite because they are easy to rent, they are equally easy to sell, and you can easily get financing. However, in many areas, rental income from SFRs- single family rentals isn't enough to provide positive cash flow.

- **Duplex/Triplex/Quads**

The multifamily properties that come with two to four units bring the best of both the financing and secure purchasing benefits right to you. These types of properties, bought correctly, allow for a good cash flow and there is not much competition compared to bidding on single family homes. These multifamily properties serve as a substantial investment and can also act as a personal resident for the newbie investor. The good thing about these kinds of units is that you only need one loan to secure 2 to 4 units on that property because the guidelines are just the same for the single family homes.

- **Small Apartments**

Small apartment buildings usually are low density and makeup about five at the minimum and 50 at the maximum. Most investors typically view a 50 unit apartment as small, although there are not defined rules to this.

Small apartment complexes are slightly harder to get financing compared to the single-family homes or the duplexes. Buildings like this rely on commercial lending rates and standards, but despite this, small apartment complexes reap in significant cash flow and are perfect for the investor who prefers to have a more hands-on approach to managing her investments.

On another note, competition is lower when it comes to properties like these because they are too small for professional and large REITs to invest in and on the other hand, too large for most newbie investors.

Small apartment buildings value is based on the income they channel in, which results in a significant opportunity for the investor to add value by ways of increasing rental, decreasing expenses and proper management. These properties require on-site managers who will be able to manage and perform necessary performance in exchange for decreased or even a free rental.

- **Large Apartments**

Large apartments refer to complexes that are common in many countries and boast plenty of amenities such as pools, gyms, sauna and a full management office. Some also come with mini convenience stores, a laundry, and a salon. These properties have high advertising budgets and can cost millions of dollars to purchase and are usually built at a very prominent or accessible part of town. So, with a high buying price, you can also be assured of very lucrative and stable returns with minimal personal involvement.

- **REITs**

We talked about REITs (Real Estate Investment Trust) in the previous chapter as well. REITs involve a group of individuals pooling their funds jointly and establishing a REIT, and they allow the REIT to acquire large scale real estate investments from skyscrapers, vast quantities of single family homes, large apartment complexes, shopping malls and sports complexes. When there's profit, the trust distributes the profits to the investors. REITs can be purchased via your stock account, and they usually come with a high dividend payment.

- **Commercial**

Commercial investments are categorized as property that is leased to a business, and it varies in style, size as well as purpose. Investors lease buildings to small scale local businesses while some investors prefer to rent it out to big business. Commercial properties are an excellent source of good cash flow and are always consistent on payment, but they also carry longer holding periods especially during times of vacancies. There is always the possibility of commercial properties staying vacant for an extended period, usually months or even years. This is not recommended for the novice investor unless you are starting with an extremely solid financial foundation.

- **Vacation Homes**

Vacation homes can be acquired at sometimes a relatively low price. Depending on whether you choose to buy a time-share in a controlled and association-run park, or a single home in a residential neighborhood. Depending on the location, these can be a great source of cash flow throughout the year. It is important to know the rules of the area and the home-owner association rules when getting into this market. Not all condos are allowed to be rented out. Do your research on the area and housing situation.

- **Flipping Houses**

Flipping homes is when you buy a property that needs to be fixed up. You invest in the renovation of the property and then turn around and sell it for profit. This can be very profitable. Get to know the location, area and make sure you have the right people around you to help you when fixing it up. Quality should match the price, but there also needs to be a profit in the end. You can also decide to just rent out the house in the end and not sell it.

- **Mobile Homes**

Investing in mobile homes is a great option because it requires very little investment. Many of the strategies used in the other types of real estate investing can be applied to a mobile home, whether it's on a land of its own or in a mobile home park.

- **Tax Liens**

Tax liens are not advisable for the novice trader because it requires experience above all, as well as a little bit of research and knowledge. Tax liens happen then a property goes into foreclosure and is resold to property investors for the amount of taxes owed. This result in inexpensive properties but while the price may seem lucrative, be cautious and practice diligence before investing.

- **Notes**

Notes are paper mortgages and investing in them is the activity of buying and selling paper mortgages. A 'note' is created when a home is purchased with a loan. This note explains the terms of the contract. A note, just like any other real estate investment, is usually sold at a discount when the seller is motivated to sell. A note buyer is required for the transaction to take place, whereby the note buyer will begin collecting monthly mortgage payments. The note buyer has the right to keep the note or sell it.

Conclusion

The investment niches outlined above are some of the ways that you can start in investing in real estate. It is always useful to pick one or two niches when you are starting out and then carve your expertise in that niche. Later on, as, you go on acquiring the knowledge; you can always take on other niches and expand.

These various strategies and niches have its own strengths and benefits, depending on when you attempt to take them on during your real estate investment growth. However, before you attempt any of this, you need to learn an investment tactic that you can use for the niche of your choice. In the next section, we will look at creating or choosing your plan to make money using the niches above.

Chapter 5: Choose Your Real estate Investing Strategies

When you learn the ropes of real estate investing, it isn't just enough to know the various niches available. You must, as a keen and success-oriented investor, learn to use these different tactics when dealing with niches to create your wealth.

Here are three universal strategies that you can exploit to make money:

Strategy 1- Buy & Hold

The 'buy & hold' strategy is the most favored kind of strategy as it involves the investor buying a property and then renting it out for an extended period. It works, it's simple, and it is the purest and easy form of real estate investing that anyone can do. The investor seeks out to generate wealth by renting the property and then amassing monthly cash flow or only holding said property until a particular time to sell it again to gain profits. The advantage of this strategy is that during the holding period of the asset, you can rent it out and the mortgage is still being paid for every month, which then decreases your principal balance while growing your equity in the property.

The buy and hold investor needs to understand one critical thing- evaluating deals and identifying opportunities. One of the most common mistakes done by property investors is that they buy bad contracts because of the lack of understanding property evaluation. Other mistakes novice investors do are making terrible decisions on tenant selection, underestimating expenses and failing to supervise their assets properly.

We will discuss these errors in another chapter, so you are aware but really- these mistakes can be avoided only by learning the ropes of the business instead of jumping into it without basic knowledge or understanding because these mistakes will cost you financially and sometimes get you into trouble with legal matters.

To successfully execute a buy and hold strategy, the investor should learn to expertly spot the tide of the market in which is property is classified in. What the investor should look out for is to study market conditions when the properties they are interested in are low in prices but have a high inventory- this is when it is the right time to purchase these properties.

When the market is over-heated, investors with experience usually stop buying until the market settles back down. These are called slow periods, and the investor may choose to sell or continue to hold properties.

There are occasions when an investor never actually sells a property, instead wants to pay the mortgage off and live on the cash flow, and then selling the property as 'Seller Financing.'

When it comes to the buy and hold strategy, there is much more than meets the eye. The good thing is that if you continue to learn how to evaluate market conditions and property prices, you'll also be able to buy better deals, manage your property better, find quality tenants and ultimately create a successful route towards your real-estate investment business.

Strategy 2- Flipping Real Estate

Flipping houses have become popular in recent times thanks to many shows on TV such as 'Flip or Flop' and 'Fixer Upper, ' and it is one of the popular tricks of the real estate trade in making money. Flipping houses is the practice of purchasing a real estate property at a relatively discounted price and then improving or renovating it for the purpose of selling it for profit. This house flipping model is very similar to the 'buy low and sells high' model practiced in retail businesses.

Single-family homes are the most common and preferred property types of flipping. A knowledgeable house flipper will usually pay for a home following the 70% rule whereby a house is purchased for 70% of its current value. Say if a home is worth $200,000 and requires at least $20,000 worth of repairs and renovations to be done. The expert house flipper will purchase the house for $120,000 ($200,000 x 70% - $20,000) and set out to sell the house at $200,000 when the renovations have been completed.

This is just a simple equation to give you an idea of how it works. In reality, these actual numbers are verified and adjusted in real time to ensure that the flip is fruitful and profitable.

Speed is an essential aspect in house flipping. The expert house flipper will endeavor to buy, renovate and sell the said property as fast as possible to guarantee a highest profitability and to steer clear of any expensive carrying costs. These carrying costs come in the form of monthly bills such property taxes, financing charges as well as maintenance or condo costs that are required to keep the house in proper financial standing. Flipping only guarantees cash flow when an investor continues flipping houses. Cash flow stops when they stop flipping too.

Strategy 3- Wholesaling Real Estate

The act of wholesaling is the activity of sourcing out fantastic real estate contracts, lettering a contract to obtain that particular deal and then selling the contract to another interested purchaser. A wholesaler doesn't actually own the property they are selling, but instead, the wholesaler procures these amazing deals through a variety of marketing tactics. Once he finds it, he puts them under contract and then sells the contract to another person for an 'assignment fee.' Sound dubious, but this is perfectly legal. This fee is anywhere within the range of $500 to 5,000, and it can increase depending on the size of the deal. The wholesale is actually the middleman who is paid to find these lucrative deals.

Most wholesalers sell their contracts to other investors, who are usually house flippers and who are typical 'cash buyer's but some wholesalers prefer dealing with retail buyers. Ultimately, when dealing with cash buyers, a wholesaler can expect to be paid within a short period, usually within days or weeks and this also results in a substantial connection within the real estate community.

Wholesaling is often a preferred method for investors because of the reputation that it comes with – an easy strategy that comes with low startup costs especially when you first beginning. There are no rehab costs or loan fees, tenants, contracts to deal with, banks and other issues because the property is never actually owned by the wholesaler. While all these may sound very easy, it, however, isn't as easy to become a wholesaler that is successful.

Being a wholesaler means that you have to continually seek out the best deals around your region to ensure a consistent stream or great deals to sell to others and this, of course, requires a robust, extensive network to continually attract these deals.

This is a strategy that is wildly promoted as something anyone can do in the property market with absolutely no monetary investment. But in reality, you do need financial resources to build your marketing needs. Persistence and perseverance are required in this strategy to grow your wholesaling skills and find success as well as a steady stream of income.

Chapter 6: Resources & Tools for the Newbie Investor

The great thing about being an investor in our modern, internet-connected world is that there is growing information when it comes to anything you want to learn. With all that information available at your fingertips, it's hard to pinpoint what information is paramount and useful and what information just wastes your time.

It isn't wrong to digest all the information you can get. Experience combined with trial and error will teach you which ones you will find useful. It's understandable to be confused and not know where to start when you begin your real estate investing journey but starting somewhere is a must. Every day is a new learning opportunity, and with being in the 21st century, you get to derive information from not only through books or seminars, but you also have handy tools that you can use just by using your smartphone by way of apps.

From apps to internet tools, web tools to books, try the various tools and see which of these works for you. Every investor has their personal finance philosophy, and you'd have tailored your own too. By educating yourself on all the various ways of investing in real estate, you not only minimize your risk of making mistakes and losses, but you also become more confident in making the right choices and the direction you want to take in your investing.

Here are some of those tools that you can use to help you that have been tried and tested. Again, it may not be something you're looking for, but it's worth trying. Some tools can change your life and create the impact you need. Whether they are free apps, websites, books and mentors, each of these components helps shape your perception in investing and help you grow.

Books that expand your mind

Perseverance and consistency, as well as knowledge, is a potent combination when you invest in something- be it a skill, technique, an object. Along the path to success, it is easy to be discouraged or think of giving up. That's when books come in. Books written by people who have been through what you are going through or rags to riches story, overcoming all odds can be an influential mentor to you. It can open your eyes to opportunities you never saw in the first place.

Read as much as you can and as quickly as you possibly can. Some books need to be read multiple times to fully grasp its content. Sometimes you also need to read it again especially when you feel like you're going through the same thing. Expanding your knowledge should be a consistent effort because things are always changing around you and so, educating yourself constantly is needed as well. Here are some books to help you in your real estate investment journey:

- [Think and Grow Rich](#) by Napoleon Hill

- [Rich Dad Poor Dad](#) by Robert Kiyosaki

- [A Random Walk down Wall Street](#) by Burton Malkiel

- [Smart Women Finish Rich](#) by David Bach

- [The Power Of Real Estate Investing](#) by Kemi Egan

In real estate investing, it isn't useful to only understand the stock market. It's good to know other periphery industries and market conditions to help you make better and more informed decisions. Expanding your financial and property knowledge is essential because guess what, the financial market always changing and there's always new ideas created.

Blogs that Blow your Mind

Apart from books, there's always blogs that get updated instantly with any new investing trends so follow your favorite blogs too. Here are some really great blogs that you can follow:

- http://www.thebigpictureblog.com/

The Big Picture is managed by the Chief Investment Officer of a financial planning firm- Barry Ritholtz. He covers various topics under investing and trading from macroeconomics to rental evaluation and everything else in the property market. He has 130 million visitors a month and has also written a book called 'Bailout Nation' now available on Amazon.

- http://www.goodfinancialcents.com/

Jeff Rose talks about personal finance advice on his blog and he is also the CEO of his own wealth management firm. Jeff has experienced failure (you can read about his street cred on his blog) in immense degrees as well as success, which make him very relatable to the common man. Jeff is also an author of personal finance book 'Soldier of Finance'.

- http://moneynomad.com/

The Money Nomad is focused on providing information and tips for people looking to start their very own online business. The primary goal of the Money Nomad is to make money online. He writes topics on online businesses, investing as well as finance. The Money Nomad is run by primary blogger Rod and often features contributed articles from like-minded people.

- http://thecollegeinvestor.com/

The College Investor is run by Robert Farrington who is determined in helping millennials build real wealth for their future. He also writes about managing student loans and debts and provides tips on how to manage millennial investing and achieve financial freedom. There are also a bunch of free tools from this website that can be used for banking, personal finance, and investing.

- https://investorjunkie.com/

The Investor Junkie's primary content is geared towards making a smarter investor and entrepreneur out of their readers. Larry Ludwig is the editor and brings in a depth of knowledge in everyday investing experience. Investor Junkie is where you can get unbiased financial advice and smart tips in managing your personal finance.

- http://retireby40.org/

It all started with Joe Udo's goal of retiring by the age of 40 and he did all that by being frugal and making extremely smart investment choices which he now shares in his blog. This blog guides readers in making informed financial and investment decisions that will help you save money faster. If retiring early is your goal, then follow Joe's blog.

- http://awealthofcommonsense.com/

Author and founder of A Wealth of Common Sense, Ben Carlson breaks down the various elements of financing to give you a simplified version that anyone can understand. This blog focuses on financial markets, wealth management, investor psychology as well as investment types.

Apps That Build Positive Investing Habits

Apps are a great tool that can help you create and track useful and positive financial habits and most of these apps are readily downloaded either free or with very minimal fee directly to their smartphones. These financial apps help novice to experienced investors to plan and budget and invest in workable financial strategies. Again, find the app that works for you and your lifestyle.

Developing proper financial habits is extremely important in growing a healthy investment portfolio. Whether it is saving to purchase your very first property or building your retirement fund, you need to be consistent and stay on track. Your consistency will be rewarded in due time. Here are some of the great apps to try:

- **Tip Yourself**

Tip Yourself is an application that helps anyone develop positive financial habits. It is based on a positive reinforcement where you reward yourself when you have a positive life experience when you achieve a goal you created. For example, if your goal was to save $500 at the end of the month, you reward yourself by treating yourself to a nice dinner or if your goal was to work out 4 times a week, then you reward yourself by a little retail therapy. You can also connect the app to your social network or fellow users so you can encourage each other to reach their goals

Saving money is one of the key actions in your investing journey and it is a great stepping stone to create and develop positive habits.

- **Acorn**

Acorn allows the novice investor to invest your spare change. This is another great app that can create positive financial habits. The thing about Acorn is that it teaches you to save from 50 cents to 5 dollars- you'd be surprised how small change here and there can add up over time.

It also teaches you not to be wasteful with your extra money.

- **Property Fixer**

Property Fixer is great for the investor who wants to flip and wants a sure fire way to quickly analyze any potential profit in a house that they intend to fix and flip. The app allows you to input the address, size of the property, a photo, a description as well as any expenses such as holding costs, renovation and repair costs and so on. From the data that has been inputted, the app calculates the profit margin as well as the return of investment.

- **Zillow**

Very much like the website, the app can be downloaded to your smartphone and pull up an impressive amount of data on real estate. You can check the price of homes for sale or see nearby competitive properties, forecasted rental rates and so on.

- **The Landlord App**

If you have various rental properties of your own and you need to keep track of everything- then you'll like this app. It puts all information of your properties right onto your smartphones so that it is easily accessible anytime, anywhere. You can easily keep track of tenants who have not paid their rents; you can also upload postings directly onto Craigslist and also keep track of your portfolio's financial performance. This app is great for landlords who are on the go as it helps you organize everything without you having to carry binders and papers.

Investing Tools to Help Define Your Money Philosophy

Apart from apps and books, you also have options to stay on track with web applications.

- **Wealthfront**

With Wealthfront, you have an easily accessible and competent platform to invest your money in. Wealthfront allows anyone with enough experience to access long-term investment options with very little fees involved. The

Wealthfront team is backed by experts in the investing area that can help you navigate your investing journey. This is a great platform for first-time investors as well.

- **Betterment**

Betterment is another easy platform that makes it even easier to manage all your accounts and automate investment efforts. This platform makes your investing simple and not overwhelming for novice investors. You can manage your finances pretty easily with the effective automation tool that makes this platform stand out from the rest.

- **Real Estate Calculator**

The [investment property calculator](#) makes calculating numbers on your investment property simpler and easier. It helps you identify a good deal from a bad one by giving you crucial operating ratios such as the DSCR (Debt Service

Coverage Ratio), NOI (Net Operating Income), NIM (Net Income Multiplier), CAP (Capitalization Ratio), and more.

The handy calculator in the sidebar also adds up numbers as you go through inputting required data.

- **Connected Investors**

If you want to expand your knowledge, meet other industry players, competitors even and just generally grow your network, Connected Investors is a great place to start in. This is a great site for property research as well as for buying and selling properties. What's unique about it is that is has a vibrant and rich community- both in dollars as well as in knowledge. The community's entire focus is for successful real estate investing.

Conclusion

Whether it's a mobile app, a book or a web tool, you can use these different varieties to help you navigate yourself in the world of real estate investing. Not only will it teach you to make better financial habits, it will also help you create your own philosophy on money. The bottom line is to find what works for you. So you don't have to just stick to one tool- make use of a variety of tools for various investing or savings needs- just like how you use various social network platforms to get your message out.

Using these tools doesn't really require a high-end computer or tech skills. All it needs is a working internet connection, a smartphone and yes of course- your laptop or personal computer. Log onto these apps or websites and find the best ways to calculate, assess, evaluate and forecast your property.

Chapter 7: How to Avoid Common Mistakes Newbie Investors Make

The first time for anything you set out to do is usually either difficult or awkward, and you're not sure whether you are doing it right. It's the same with investing as well. Your first deal is usually difficult to obtain or to close because you don't know enough and don't worry - no one is expecting you to be born knowing everything related to investing anyway.

But when it is time you set yourself up to spend, that's when you need to learn and absorb as much as you can. Your first deal may not be perfect, but it is a step in the right direction. Even if it isn't entirely accurate, any novice investor hates for the deal to be so bad that it makes recovering from it incredibly hard or just push you out of the playing field. In this chapter, we will look at the various mistakes that novice real estate investors do and how to avoid them. Knowing these mistakes will help you avoid worst case possibilities.

Mistake #1- Bad Financing

Bad financing ruins pretty much a lot of things we get ourselves in whether it's buying a new home, buying a new car, moving jobs, investing in a business, investing in education, starting a new career or even starting a new family.

In real estate investing, bad financing is a lethal mistake that is the number one reason that causes investors to lose money and go out of business quicker than you can say 'I've done it!'

What is bad financing? It isn't just about having little capital. Bad financing is a combination of:

- High monthly payments
- High interest rates

- Balloon payment

- Adjustable interest rate

- Personal recourse

Mortgages from residential banks save you from making the mistakes from high-interest rates, adjustable interest rates, high monthly payments and balloon payments only because these banks have low-interest rates, are fixed for 30 years, and there are no balloons because of amortizing payments.

However, like all banks, they also require personal recourse which means you need to personally guarantee the loan with your current assets and future earnings. Personal recourse is a legal agreement where the lender has full legal rights to pledge collateral in the scenario that the borrower is unable to fulfill the debt obligation. The lender has the legal right to collect.

This is a reasonable trade-off with residential banks. Other banks, however, aren't so kind. Commercial, portfolio, hard money and private lenders do not meet any of the criteria listed above, and if this is your first deal, it could pose a colossal problem.

When you borrow at 12% interest with a large monthly payment, you are looking at a balloon that is due in one to three years, and you are mostly taking too much of a risk when there's a full personal recourse for the loan. Why is this a risk- because the property comes with a negative cash flow with a high-interest rate. The balloon note means you will have to refinance or sell your property in a short period.

Many investors learned this during the 2008 credit crisis and tried refinancing when their credit dried up. But this is tough to do at this financial crisis even when you have perfect credit and reasonably good income. When it comes to personal recourse, this means that if anything goes bad and your lender loses money, they can chase you to repay to recover their lost money and also take away your other assets to collect.

For real estate deals, it is always good to use plenty of private and seller financing schemes. The good thing about private funding is that everything is negotiable. So no matter what type of financing you choose to use, just make sure to negotiate and avoid worst case mistakes.

Mistake #2- Bad Location

Location, location, location- real estate value is all about location. The individuals and businesses wanting to rent or buy your property will first look into the location, and the other criteria are considered once they are satisfied with the location. As a novice investor, starting out at the area that you are familiar with is essential. Starting out at the area that you are familiar with makes it easier for you to identify the best locations and the bad ones, so you will know which ones to buy.

It's not to say that you will not make money at all in bad locations- you will but it takes time to understand what and how that property can contribute to its surroundings and the economy and community around it. Attracting good tenants at a bad location will also be problematic even if the price is right.

Mistake #3- Misjudging Resale or Rent Value

One of the primary roles of a real estate investor is to understand how our customers- who are potential tenants or potential property buyers make decisions when buying property. This will help the investor add value to the property and also make better property buying decisions. If you as investors cannot determine the full value of the asset, then it will be a harder process of making a confident purchase that can turn into a profit. Evaluating a property needs experience, and this is something you need to commit to learn and refine every time for the rest of your career in real estate investment. While you may not be an expert on value at your first deal, there are a few things that you can do to produce a better investment result:

- Decrease the size of your target market to a manageable area

- Study the various transactions in your market as often as you can, daily even, using various tools such as Zillow, MLS, and even your local tax assessor. This keeps you on updated on any changes or updates in your property target market.

- Hire professionals if you must. Get help from real estate agents or appraisers to find the value of properties and their rental rates.

- Take courses and classes on valuation

Mistake #4: Underestimating Repair Costs

At some point in your real estate career, you will make the mistake of underestimating repair costs. Of course, the more experienced you get, the wiser you become incorrectly estimating how much repair and renovations will cost to your property.

As novice investors, you want to avoid massive overrun costs that may result in you running out of cash or running into other problems. To prevent huge mistakes, you need to learn repair costs as well and refine your estimating skills. Again, this is where getting help will come in handy. If you have connections or friends who work or own repair or renovation services, get them to help you estimate the costs. You can also get some good advice from your mentors (refer to chapter 1) as well as other contractors whom you trust for advice.

Contractors, real estate agents, property managers and even bank employees are good connections to have in your network, and they will be your go-to person to seek advice and assistance should you ever need some pointers.

Mistake #5: Running Out of Cash

This mistake relates to mistake #1 as well. Your property is your baby and your cash is the food. When you run out of food, your baby dies. Morbid story but that's how it'll be when you do run out of cash. Even the best property on the investment market will hurt your wealth creation when you do not have enough fuel. Here are some possible reasons why this usually happens:

- You underestimated the cost of repairs (see mistake #3)

- You underestimated future capital expenses on property rentals

- You started off with bad financing (see mistake #1)

Capital expenses are such as replacing your heating system or installing new tiles or painting the entire house. If you did not estimate the cost of this, you're running into a huge problem.

Mistake #6: Letting Emotions Drive Your Decisions

Ah yes- the use of emotions when investing. It is totally understandable that you feel emotions on your real estate investing career. It is exciting and thrilling as it is frustrating and stressful. The thing is you need to balance your enthusiasm with objective analysis each time, every time. As an entrepreneur, enthusiasm is essential as it keeps you going no matter the obstacles you face. But when making financial decisions, learn to never make them with your emotions alone.

Making big financial decisions requires a process of analysis and you also need to run these deals by your mentor and advisors. Begin with the basic criteria such as location, neighborhood, construction quality, ease of access as well as housing type. This will help you filter down the huge list of properties available out there.

Mistake #7: Choosing the Wrong Real Estate Strategy

Real estate investing has many strategies and you must choose strategies that work for you and the property you are investing in. Here's a great tip- you will not find the perfect one-size-fits-all strategy but you can find one that suits your unique qualities and skills for both your short term and long term goals.

Instead of looking out for the perfect strategy or borrowing one from someone else (although this is not wrong), think about what it is that you really want from your investments and which real estate strategy that you've used will help get you there. Different strategies work differently with different results.

Mistake #8: Choosing Bad Contractors

Bad contractors are as damaging as bad tenants. The people you hire to renovate or repair your house will ultimately make or break your first deal success. Source out for contractors that will do a good job, clean up after themselves, finish up on time and charge reasonable prices. Your connections and mentor will be able to advise which contractor fit in the category because word of mouth is still the best advertising.

Mistake #9: Not Using Your Due Diligence Period

Some investors, usually the experienced ones often go with fast closings, in 'as-is' conditions and no due diligence period. While this may help them get a lower price on property, it is not recommended for novice investors.

A reasonable due diligence period allows you to get out of the purchase contract when there is a problem. Here are a few crucial points to look at during the due diligence period:

- Get the professional opinion of a third party property inspection
- Get repair estimates and run it by your mentor and advisors
- Evaluate zoning and local ordinances
- Get a professional third party opinion of value and rental comps

The idea behind getting opinions is that you want to double check all your estimates and assumptions before you make your offer on a property. If all opinions from your mentors and advisor point towards a bad assumption, then you may need to renegotiate or even go so far as walking away from the deal.

Mistake #10: Not Learning From Your Mistakes

Learning from your mistakes is part and parcel of life because after all, life is 'the schools of hard knocks. As much as you want to avoid mistakes, you'll make them anyway and this list is only to minimize and risk factors and make you more aware. At the end of the day, continue learning and seeking out knowledge to better equip yourself.

Conclusion

Real estate investing is a business and investors are entrepreneurs as well. To reach for the stars, you also need to take risks and these risks may or may not be so bad. Look at risks as a barrier to better beginnings. Risks make you more committed to excel and it also weeds out the investors that aren't ready to take the lap.

The successful real estate investor is not perfect but they all have taken risks and have learned from them. Eventually, the higher the stakes, the better they are to avoid these mistakes and keep moving forward.

Chapter 8: The Correct Way to Value and Analyze Investment Property

Unlike stocks, there is no straightforward way to determine the precise value of your current property or the property you plan on buying. When it comes to real estate investment, it is all about purchasing, maintaining and holding the property for as long as possible to build wealth.

In this chapter, we will look at valuing property from an investor's point of view. If you are already a property or homeowner, this is a great way of valuing your own property as realistic as possible.

Valuing Property

1) **It's all about income**

As a real estate investor, it is crucial that you establish what the practical income your desired property can produce on a consistent and sustainable foundation yearly. Historical and current income figures matter the most when evaluating. Once you can have an income range, you can then calculate a property's gross rental yield and price to earnings valuation and compare it with other similar properties within the neighborhood.

2) Price appreciation comes in second

Many investors choose to focus on potential property appreciation instead of the income component of the property which is one of the main reasons why there was a housing bubble in the first place and then a collapse ensued after. Investors weren't bothered about the massive cash flow negative knowing that they could rally on and still flip a property for profits within a year. The real problem came when the property bubble burst and caused a crash, resulting in a domino effect. This hurt the prospects of first-time buyers who were planning to buy and hold. When investors look at only property appreciation and not its income- they become a spectator. But there is no validity in real estate investment if there is not generating of revenue.

3) Property prices historically increase closely with inflation

The appreciation of property prices follows inflation closely by +/- 2%. For example, if the inflation is 3% then expect property prices nationwide to increase at 1 – 5%. Property price changes can fluctuate madly over the years. If you look closely at property prices over a period of 10 years, you'll notice that there's a relatively smooth correlation. The thing is, some investors become delusional when they start having prospects for consistent 10% annual value gains. Remember that property price appreciation should be a secondary attribute, not the ultimate goal. If there's a profit- excellent but always just focus on your cash flow.

4) Property is always local

Do not generalize property statistics just because in one report it says that property prices in the California are up 10.5% in June year after year that does not mean you'll get to sell your property for 10.5% more. You cannot generalize national property statistics either. The best way to find out what the value of your home is, it is when your neighbor sells their property. Property prices in reports give you a general idea of the direction of prices and the relative areas of strength.

Additional Steps to Value your Property Correctly

1) Calculating your yearly gross rental income

Use a practical monthly market rent based on comparable figures you can find on the internet and times that by 12 to get your annual rent. From here, take the gross annual rent and divide it by the market rate of your property.

For instance:

- $3000/month= $36,000/year

- $36,000/500,000= 7.2% gross rental yield.

The gross rental yield is to give you an apple to apple comparison of what potential is available for a property if you were to pay 100% cash and have absolutely no other ongoing expenses.

2) Comparing gross rental yield to the risk-free rate

The risk-free rate refers to the 10-year bond yield. The word 'risk-free' is given by investors because there is zero chance that the US government will default on their debt obligations. All investment require a risk premium over the risk-free rate because if not, there is no point risking your money by investing it at all. If the annual gross rental yield of the property is much lower than the risk-free rate, then you need to bargain harder or just move on from the deal.

3) Calculating your annual net rental yield

Net rental yield refers to your net operating income, divided by the market value of your property. You can calculate your net operating income by taking your annual gross rent and then subtracting the mortgage interest, property taxes, HOA dues, insurance as well as maintenance and marketing costs. In other words, what you are doing is calculating the actual bottom line annual profit.

Calculating a Real Estate Property's Net Operating Income

$$\text{Market Value} = \frac{NOI_1}{r-g} = \frac{NOI_1}{R}$$

Where:

- NOI - net operating income

- r - Required rate of return on real estate assets

- g- Growth rate of NOI

- R- Capitalization rate (r-g)

You can also add in depreciation rates but for the time being, just focus on cash flow. For instance:

$24,000/year in rent - ($3,000/year HOA dues, $4,800/year property taxes, $500/year insurance, $1,000/year maintenance, $10,000 in mortgage interest after tax adjustments)

= $4,700 NOP. $4,700/$500,000 = 1% net rental yield.

This is not so good but on the bright side, at lease you have positive cash flow from the get go. Net rental yield differs between investors depending on how much money they put in.

4) Comparing the net rental yield to the risk-free rate

You want the net rental yield to be equivalent or higher than the risk-free rate. You will need to pay the principal down as time goes by which will then increase the net rental yield and spread the risk-free rate. If everything goes well, the rent will also go up, and your property price will appreciate. Properties in Nevada, California, Florida and Arizona have net rental yields that are several percentage points higher than their current risk-free rate, even after the collapse. There is the reason why more and more people did not snatch up property between 2010 to 2012 because buyers we requested to pay in cash as the banks weren't giving out any loans.

5) Calculating the price to earnings ratio of your property

The Price to Earnings ratio is basically the market value of your property which is then divided by the current net operating profit. Say for instance:

$500,000 / $4,700 = 106.

This would mean the owner of the property needs 106 years of net operating profits to get his or her investment back. This is of course under the assumption that the owner never pays down the mortgage and does not see an increase in rents- a situation which is highly unlikely. A better way to calculate this is to get the gross rental income and then divide it by the market value of the property. For instance:

$500,000 / $24,000 = 20.8

Obviously, the lower the P/E for the buyer, the better, and vice versa for the seller.

6) Forecast property price and rental expectations

The price to earnings ratio and the rental yields are only short term outlooks. The real opportunity is when expectations are properly forecasted. As a real estate investor, you want to take advantage of fear and unfortunate situations whereas as a real estate seller, you want to take advantage of selling a dream of prices that are forever rising. The best way to forecast property is to compare what has happened in the past by analyzing data and online charts which you can find in places like Zillow, Trulia, and DataQuick. They will give you a realistic expectation of the local employment growth and tell you whether businesses are moving or leaving the city. It'll also give you a good idea of the land provided by the city for development and any building restrictions such as the height of buildings and land space.

7) Run various scenarios

The final way of valuating your property would be to obtain a realistic property price as well as rental forecast and run in through various possible scenarios. If rental prices decrease for five years at a rate of 5% each year, will you be OK with that? If mortgage rates for 30-year fixed loans increase from 2.5% to 5.5% in five years, how will that affect the demand for property?

If the principal value declines to another 23%, will that make you stressed out? Always run a bullish case, a realistic case, and a bearish case scenario to test your bare minimum.

8) Keep a wary eye on taxes and depreciation

Remember that all kinds of expenses concerning ownership of a rental property is taxable and this is inclusive of property taxes and mortgage interest rates. The problem lies in the phase-out of deductions based on your income. Another thing to understand is depreciation which is a non-cash item that may reduce your Net Operating Income (depreciation is a noncash cost) to decrease your returns but also your tax bill.

Be focused on the actual bottom line cash in the end. For example, individuals with profits of $250,000 and married couples with earnings of $500,000 are un-taxable if you live in your property for two out of five years. There is also the 1031 exchange which enables investors to turn over proceeds to another property without any profits and only taxes. This tax code is confusing, but the margins favor property owners.

9) Check comparable sales

One of the easiest ways to check on comparable sales over the past six to 12 months would be to look up the address of a property using Zillow. At Zillow, you would be able to see the tax records, sales history as well as comparables. Use the site to compare your target property's selling price with previous sales and measure it against the factors that have changed to make sure you get a good deal.

Valuing Property- part guessing game part science

The more transactions and open houses you religiously follow from start to end, the more comfortable you will be with your ability to access property values. It will become second nature to you to identify whether a property is a bad or good deal. Valuating property is essential in the real estate investment game because it will lead to success or failure. Failure is good as it's a lesson but a failure that takes so long to repair and pushes you out the game is something you want to avoid.

If you are a novice investor looking to buy your first property or a seasoned investor looking to expand, visiting weekly open houses for a few months before putting down your purchase is essential to get the feel of your local area and market.

Property investment must always be viewed as a long-term investment because of its high selling costs of 5 to 6% commission levels, and it is always worth doing your research and understanding and checking prices online.

Properties are tangible assets, unlike stocks which lose their value in a millisecond for a variety of reasons. Can you think of any other asset category that enables you to live substantially for free has a positive effect on its value and makes a profit without you stressing too much especially if you can have the funds for the mortgage payments?

Conclusion

Thank for making it through to the end of *Real Estate Investing*, let's hope it was informative and able to provide you with all of the tools you need to achieve your goals whatever it may be.

How you evaluate and determine property prices includes various factors together with an objective analysis of fact-based data from the property's physical characteristics to the final sale price.

Investors buy and sell real estate, and because we are all humans and not machines, there are idiosyncrasies and quirks that come into play which can affect valuation and perception.

If you do not take into consideration skillful negotiation and seasonality, then it is possible that your house may never sell or even if it does, then it could be a rate that is significantly lesser than the property's true market value.

Highly skilled and experienced real estate investors bring much more to the table than just buying and selling a property and collecting rent. Determining the property value and correctly analyzing it is a multifaceted process that when executed properly, will bring the investor gains and minimize any potential losses

So remember- find your niche, seek advice from your mentors, continue to enhance your skills and increase your knowledge in the real estate investment world and refine your evaluation skills.

Thanks again for buying my book. If you have a minute, please leave a positive review.

Leave your review. Thank you!

I take reviews seriously and always look at them. This way, you are helping me provide you better content that you will LOVE in the future. A review doesn't have to be long, just one or two sentences and a number of stars you find appropriate (hopefully 5 of course).

Also, if I think your review is useful, I will mark it as "helpful." This will help you become more known on Amazon as a decent reviewer, and will ensure that more authors will contact you with free books in the future. This is how we can help each other.

DISCLAIMER: This information is provided "as is." The author, publishers and/or marketers of this information disclaim any loss or liability, either directly or indirectly as a consequence of applying the information presented herein, or in regard to the use and application of said information. No guarantee is given, either expressed or implied, in regard to the merchantability, accuracy, or acceptability of the information. The pages within this book have been copyrighted.

www.ingramcontent.com/pod-product-compliance
Lightning Source LLC
Chambersburg PA
CBHW030910180526
45163CB00004B/1782